DECADES OF LYRICAL VERSE

JOE WECKERLE

For Kate,
Our Snow Angel
WLY!

This joyous effort is also for all those who've
passed through my life and passed on, and to
those who remain by my side.

You are my daily inspiration.

Table of Contents

Foreward

This collection of poems/songs represents my perspective at different times of my life. So many things impact us daily and we all have our opinions that shape who we become. It's an ever-changing process that has always served as inspiration for me as a writer. It is truly a blessing to be able to put words on paper that capture the moment so vividly.

Enjoy!

Joe Weckerle
November 11, 2016

Don't Make Faces (Circa 1970)

Nature has started to vomit
She is being gaged by pollution
Smokestacks down her throat
Like huge tongue depressors
Nature's gurgling on detergent
She cries out at being trampled
By poor feet and rich feet
If she leaves
We have to go alone,
But, there is no alone
Without nature—
The population squirms
But feels little pain
Just smile with gritty teeth
In dirty rain
While little wars
Destroy some people
And nature takes them in...
Until she belches,
One more time
Throwing dead men up
Bomb shelters can't save us.
To know a man is to know an ass,
Who talks (but can't carry much).

JOE WECKERLE

The Stones in the Seats Are Playing Our Song

The silent movies in sin dark rooms
Just the thoughts of those who watch
Fill in the void, replace the sound.
No one talks about the hush
A smoking cigarette held tight
By the man who's in here every night.
Figures flicker in black and white
Sometimes funny, sometimes not
But no one moves or coughs out loud.
You must be deaf to hear a noise
"Where are the words?"
An audience of stifled throats
Scream deep into the theatre seats
"We write the words!"
The air was struck with mute applause
Like leather hands on soft black clay
The time has come to stop the show.
An idea squirmed out from the hole
Some unplugged ear had let it go
"The movie has gone on too long."
The only dread that swept the house
More terrible than hearing sound,
The figures on the screen might die
And the shadows have to talk...

JOE WECKERLE

Everybody Shall Be Relieved

Last day, I'm gonna sit back and look.

Everybody gonna cry while I'm dyin'.

And if it gets too loud,

I'm gonna tell 'em all.

Tell 'em what I ve done they don t know about.

Gonna quiet things down.

Everybody gonna cry while I'm dyin .

But they'll sigh when I m dead...

JOE WECKERLE

My Insight, Lamenting Nature

Colored stones in
Shiny wheather,
Falling upward,
Smell of leather.
Heaven tried it,
Found it guilty,
Watched it smiling,
Cold and filthy—
Drift apart,
Colliding boldly,
Time unscathed,
Reacts so coldly—
Falling far
From facts forsaken,
Love that's here,
Will soon be taken
For granted...

JOE WECKERLE

Winter-ling

Very few cars
Noise level very low
Just the snow
My feet are eager
For a place to go
I feel the earth,
Hard crust buried
And will be
For at least
Another month
Walking and staring,
Blinded by the paradox
Of warm sunshine
On a white cold day
Soon the houses
Will empty
The first go out
And everything
Regains it position
In this scheme
Called progress
While I
Like clothes
Go out of season.

JOE WECKERLE

Saving the World!

Imagine Jesus saying,
You are wrong.
with his scraggly beard
and dirty feet,
you wouldn t
listen...
If there were scars
upon his arms,
would you guess
they were from
needles?

What if
he walked
like a man
of the street,
must he
be stupid?

Would his message
of love
and
helping each other
be ignorant

idealism?
Would we
inform him
that things
are not that way?

Instead
of a cross
to carry,
would you
put him away,
to make
the streets safe
for the sane?

It just doesn t
make sense...
saving
the people?

When you
are crazy,
you can t
see the truth
for yourself—

Perplexed (Yet Sexual)

There she stood
like some sex-queen,
goddess bitch
of the Nile—
I could watch
her move
all night,
with those hips
that sang to me,
like the sirens
to Ulysses—

Everything
about her
spoke of instincts
that have kept
our race
alive.
I wanted to
push myself
on top of her
and breathe
some life
into her eyes,

JOE WECKERLE

(as green as the sea,
but cold as
her depths)—
the girl
has been down
once too often
for my money–

I waited
for the smoke
to clear
and made my way home.
still there she was,
stuck to me
like my reputation–

As she licked my ear,
I realized how
a blind owl
can find his nest.

A Man...A Child

A man plays games to lose his mind
To lose it though he must be quick
For minds work fast and soon they'll stick
Then never can you find
The way to lose it, far behind—
A child plays games because they re games
And he can tell you all the names
But that won t help you out.
His games leave room for doubt
While doubt is why you play the games
That does not bother you—
A man's no fool, he'll change the rules
Eventually, he's bound to win
And bound he is while choking, too
On all his rules of thumb—
A normal man has intellect (that makes him proud)
While animals must whine and howl, he can talk out loud.
But not too very long ago he could not speak at all—
He cried just like an animal and only could he crawl
Finally, he's lost it all, everything he ever had
While everything was not so bad,

JOE WECKERLE

It somehow made him sad inside.

But still he'll tell you all the names, of every childhood game,

Yet, never will he find a way to lose them far behind—

Existential Love

My memory escapes me now
I thought I knew but wasn't sure.
Yet, it will all work out somehow
Our bodies can endure.

But can and will are separate things
And we cannot ask why.
When happiness and joy still sings,
To live is but to die.

JOE WECKERLE

Senseless

The test of a man who thinks
is part of our existence.
We feel that we are ready
any time, any place, any where
we are chosen—
Some days are better than others
AND
Our test may come
on a bad day.
HOW we react
in that instant
can change lives forever—
The gun lies on the table,
cold and black staring.
It is also a test.
Some never need the gun,
leaving it for those who do.
Yet, some use it before the test.
Why not try before you die?
The bloody face once smiled,
once laughed, once cried,
once lived then died
and thought of a million things
to see, to do...

JOE WECKERLE

Victim (The Great Flood - 1913)

It rained for days
And the river swelled
The current was strong
But the old dam held.

We floated boats
In the gutter
Near the front
Of the school.
Almost everyone around
Acted pretty near a fool.

Later, someone saw a shoe
And a little sock was found.
Whoever lost those tiny things
Must certainly have drowned.
Then little Jimmy Marshall
Came floating upside down—

The water left much later,
The streets were washed,
Like new.
While sorting out the rubble
They found his small dog, too.

JOE WECKERLE

Our Mother

Out Mother was a virgin,
'Til she gave birth to my brother and me—
She learned to be a parent,
But it couldn't hide the misery.
Our Mother was an artist,
Her still-life hangs in my living room—
She painted in the evening,
It helped cover up the gloom.

All the time she was smiling,
A vacant look in her eyes.
I never thought she was dying,
In disguise...

Our Mother was a healer,
Working nights as a Registered Nurse—
She slept in the daytime,
That's when things went from bad to worse.

Our Mother was a junkie,
Got a taste for Rx pills.
It made life kinda crazy,
The bottles sat on the window sill—
Our Mother died a pauper,

JOE WECKERLE

When they turned off the breathing machine.
They called to inform us,
No one there, to make a scene—

You know they said, "It's for the best,"
Because she suffered so much.
Now she's lying, with all the rest,
Out of touch...

Our Mother was a novel, The End—

The Push

Sleeping the sleep
Of the just
Dense fog
Rolling slowly
Into the harbor,
Just one slip
Away
From free falling
Headlong
Into history
And
As always,
I leave this world
Behind
Where black
And gray
Fade into colors
You can taste,
And the dreams
I dream
All end in red
As I melt (quickly)
Inside my head
Instead

The sound
Of rushing water
Turning warmth
To ice
As my heart
Strains
To beat
While
Your firm body
Moves into
My space
Full lips brushing
(against)
My face
I must address
This love thing
Internally
Now overwhelmed
By the distance
Between us
I begin
To struggle
With euphoria
In the sincere
Belief
That we will

Stay this high
Forever
But—
This too fades
As I nod
Blissfully
Into another
State of mind
Once again
We find ourselves
(Walking the streets
Of regret)
Tonight you turn
To me
And smile
Longing to reach
Inside
My bag of tricks
For the answers
To all
Those questions
And the sky
Inside my room
Fills with
Tears of longing
For the push—

JOE WECKERLE

3761 Peaceful Place

I was not prepared
for the end.
And
even when
I collected
what was left...
it amazed me.
Despite my
utter confusion,
the irony
was clear.
She was
able to keep
up the pretense,
even after
she departed.
All was at peace
save the cat,
who lost
his best friend,
in the moment
that defined
the paradox,
which was
her life.

JOE WECKERLE

My heart
understood
what she
could never express...
This life
was too much
on most days,
but still,
she persevered
hoping for solace
and
finding comfort
in those moments
alone,
waiting for
a peaceful place
to rest,
with worry,
a thing of the past.

I love you, Kate.

Expectation(s)

The difference
between life
and death,
is a heartbeat
then silence.
That single moment
can be measured
in a million ways—
a lifetime instead
in years, months, days
And often,
we grieve
for those
who left us
behind,
to make sense
of things,
we can never
understand
completely.
Yet, there is solace
in knowing,
that real truth,
the eternal kind,

is only privy
to those
who have gone
before us,
illuminating
our way,
as we
journey
from darkness
to light.
Then
we reunite,
born again
in the blood,
assured
of the promise
that the pain
and suffering,
was worth
the price
of admission
into the lang
of consolation
and everlasting peace.
Where...
they now wait

to greet us
smiling,
restored,
complete.

JOE WECKERLE

DD

My friend,
you are ready
to move on
and
the place
is ready
for you.
It is time
to rest
your mind
and
plan for
eternity.
My daughter
will show
you around,
the place
we call
paradise.
Please keep
the light on
for the rest
of us...

I love you brother.

JOE WECKERLE

Voices (In My Distant Past)

As I drive
Along
The river
Where the train tracks
Used to be
And
The trestle
Remnant stands
Alone
Like a skeleton
That haunts
The surrounding hills...
I swear
Some nights
The whistle
Still echoes
Like
The midnight freight
From Springfield
That ran
All those years
Ago
Back when
It all made sense...

Though your
Voice
Is faint
Today
Those songs
We sang
As the evening
Slipped away
From childhood
To maturity
To eternity,
Still ring true
Making
Yesterday
More than
A memory
That I clutch
Tightly
As the madness
Caresses me nightly...

There Is a Plan

Many times
We sail along
And
Never stop to think
Then
Everything changes
With unexpected
Permanence
Causing sorrow
That permeates
Our being...
The tunnel is long,
Stretching
Before us
No light in sight
But
He touches our heart,
Just as
It breaks
In two...
Thinking
We have
No more tears
To cry

JOE WECKERLE

We stare
At what
Is left
To do
And
Dry our eyes
Pushing on
Toward
The next
Destiny
Knowing surely
This truth
Our God
Will always
Lift us up
And over
The debris
Illuminating
Our path
Until
We reunite
With our
Angels
That went
Before...

Random Gifts (Giving It All Away)

Sorting out
My life
Before departure,
Has become an exercise
In fulfilling a destiny,
With many
Varied options—
Finding room
For these tokens
Of my appreciation
For past lives
Are mixed like emotions,
Pulling me
In all directions—
As I always
Come back to you
And
The moment of truth
When we had no answers—
While the questions
Remain to haunt
The empty spaces
Between
Dusk and dawn,

JOE WECKERLE

When my glass of wine
Convinces me nightly
That I can carry
The torch for
Another day,
With visions of you,
Singing the chorus
Thats stuck in my head,
As I drive
The lonely road
That always ends
In the Graveyard
Near the train tracks
Where heaven
And earth
Once collided—

We love you, Kate

Dancing with Ricky (The Mambo Experience)

A long-time
In the making
From
A dream to
A one-page
Scheme
With
Lot of
Changes in
Dialogue
Across the pond—
The American(s)
In a foreign
Land
Standing beside
A woman (editor-in-chief)
Behind
The scenes,
Who believes
In
The man.
Driven
To make it

His way—
On a
Shoe string
Budget,
Cast
And
Crew
And
A Sony
Digital cam.
It
Was born
With a song
And we all
Came along
For the ride—
Software aside
(It took almost 2 years to post)
As he swallowed
His pride.
At the premiere
We all cheered,
Then
The smiles
Quickly faded
As reality
Set in—

While
The years
Have passed
And
So has mein freund—
I will
Always
Remember him
Fondly
For the mountain
He climbed
With the help
Of his
Woman
Who stood
In the shadows
And remains
In the distance
Silently, courageously
Smiling at
The inside joke,
His one-line
Standard,
"See you in the movies"

Das Enden
Leib always, Joe Weckerle

JOE WECKERLE

Evil Jungle Princess

Don t ever say,
you were not warned.
It says,
right on the menu...
"3 peppers Hot"
Believe it,
or suffer
the consequences...
(She ll make your heart "burn")
As you yeard
to learn,
her secret ingredient...
(Don't hold your breath!)
Pandora's Box
was a two week
vacation,
compared to
this conundrum.
Many lunches later,
you will still
be exploring
her tundra...
(not always frozen)
This aura

of mystery enhances
the dining experience—
a red wine...
instead
of dessert,completes
this gastronomic journey...
Then at last,
she smiles
(ever so slightly)
warming the room,
just before departing...
with a gentle embrace
that leaves a trace,
of perfume
And
a promise
to return,
once more,
with a recipe
for delight—

Greek Salad

Very hungry
(Almost starving)
By the harbor
At the Taverna
That we favor—
Our first lunch
Since returning
About to order—

First bread
And oil
Then the dish
That signifies
We are home
(Away from home)
A plate
Of fresh-picked
Veggies
Topped
By Feta—

Then
The traditional
First photo

Before digging
Into dreamland
The start
Of a culinary
Journey
That will last
Two weeks,
Leaving us
Forever changed
Until our
Next Holiday
In Crete—

Goat in the Oven

I see them
Everywhere
And
Hear
Their
Ringing bells—
But when
We go
To Litsa's
Place
The oven
Holds our
Climbing friend
Asleep
On a bed
Of oil
And potatoes—
Seasoned
Until golden
Delicious
On our plates
With Mythos,
Good company
And

The night
Is young.
As we
Savor
The moment
For what
Seems like
Eternity
Then
Tsikouthia
Appears
To help
Digest this
Dinner
For the ages—

High Cost of Romance

I make believe that it s over
And I m a man on my own.
Then I jump into the river,
holding a stone
You tell me that you re leaving.
I don't know what to do.
There's no time for grieving,
over you.

I still remember,
when you lit my cigarette.
Early in December,
I was almost out of debt.

You turn your back as you listen.
The words get stuck in my throat.
Your skin starts to glisten,
as you start to gloat.

It wells up inside of me.
Takes control of my thought.
I reach deep for a moment,
find the gun that you bought.

I can bear it no longer.
The irony leaps from the page.
You always were stronger.
And all I feel is rage.

I take aim at your memory.
And I envision you dead.
Though the gun isnt loaded,
it goes off in my head.

I make believe that it's over
And I'm a man on my own.
Then I jump into the river,
holding a stone...

Pirmasens Sunset

I have listened
To my feelings
As they spoke
To me of warmth
And closeness—
I've searched
Through my closets
Where I keep my
Special things—
It is there,
Somewhere deep inside
Of me,
That I found
The memories
Of you—
And much like
A movie
Of our lives,
The sounds of laughter
Run together
And paint a picture
Of those moments
Frozen in a portrait
From our past

Between
The darkness of the earth
And the shadows
Of the sky,
Where those last
Remaining images of light
Will always
Expose that fleeting sensation
Of you two, together—
Our friendship
Is as constant
As the lunar pull
Upon
The tides—
I will
Be the bridge
That brings us
Closer
To the edge,
Because you mean
The world
To me—
I love you both
So much—

Electronics Addiction

Take some advice,

Turn off your device,

They're listening to you in the valley every
night.

They know what you re drinking,

'Cos they know what you're thinking,

And deep inside you it's just not right.

Take a walk in the park,

Stay late after dark,

Enjoy the full moon high up in the sky.

Drive down a back road,

You don t need a code,

To slip away alone and escape the lie.

Maybe it's time for something new,

A drastic change in style.

So, don't look back, be calm,

'Cos it will take a while...

JOE WECKERLE

Keep dodging the flack,

You're on the right track,

The future looks bright as far as you can see.

You can handle the glare,

Just let them all stare,

It's part of the price you paid to be set free.

Take some advice,

Turn off your device,

They're listening to you in the valley every
night.

And its just not right...

A Twist (in the Tale)

Misdirection
Outright lies
Heartfelt passion
Darkened skies
Loose connection
Someone dies (tonight)

Must be something
In my drink
Like The Nothing
Start to sink
Now I'm drowning
Hard to think (in flight)

Got my number
So much more
Must get well
Have to score

Back again
Like before
Let me in
Open the door

As she closes the sale
This time I can't fail
Falling into the deep
Where no one can sleep...

Only longing for A Twist (in the Tale)

Life in a Short Film

The script says you love me
It ain't no lie.
How come every time you tell me
You can't look me in the eye?

Though we re together now
You're far away.
Well baby I'm just hopin'
The scene lasts for one more day.

Sometimes when I'm dreamin'
About the cast, it s all good.
Then I wake up screamin'
Alone in the neighborhood.

Now I'm thinkin' 'bout the ending
And it's moving way too fast.
No matter how we shoot it,
I know it just won t last.

We look so good on film,
When you're standing close to me
A kiss, then roll the credits,
It's time to face reality.

JOE WECKERLE

Axis II

16 I robbed a liquor store,
Spent 5 years in the joint,
Made a lot of license plates,
Guess I missed the point.

Shrink said I was way too cold,
Kept my feelings on a shelf,
But every time I thought of you,
I had to touch myself.

I don't know what to do,
Seems I must be ill,
I'm in lust with you.

Every night I said my prayers,
About to lose my mind,
Pain was masked by all the layers,
My thoughts were so unkind.

Thoughts of you out on the lake,
Swimming with my friends,
Shedding tears that were so fake,
And the party never ends.

JOE WECKERLE

I don't know what to do,
Seems I must be ill,
I'm in lust with you.

When I got out and took the bus,
Back to that dismal town,
With no one there to make a fuss,
And welcome home the clown.

Then I saw you on the platform,
Waiting for the train,
The air was warm, but you were cool,
The sky began to rain.

I kissed your mouth, you pulled me close,
Like so many years before,
But this time it was an overdose,
The conductor closed the door.

I don't know what to do,
Seems I must be ill,
I'm in lust with you.

Sometimes later down the line,
I can't remember where,
You produced a jug of wine,
We had one glass to share.

I made a toast to love in vain,
But vowed to get it right,
Then downed the wind to dull the pain,
Made love all through the night.

I don't know what to do,
Seems I must be ill,
I'm in lust with you.

JOE WECKERLE

Meta

Some call it a blessing
I call it a curse
The product of messing
In my small universe

And
They call me a freak of nature
While they pray for my demise
Not human but creature
Can't you see that I despise...

The gift that was bestowed on me
It will not let me die
Sentenced to eternity
With no more tears to cry

And
Yet I search for meaning
While the questions make me ill
But if I knew the answers
Would it be enough to kill...

JOE WECKERLE

This urge to make amends
For all my sins on earth
An amazing world of dead ends
That climaxed with my birth

House Full of Secrets

So many, little, dirty things,
Soap and water cannot clean.
Watches, bracelets, diamond rings,
shining darkly thin and mean.

No one home to tell the tale,
Vague whispers down the hall.
Locked up tight like the county jail,
with no where else to fall.

Don't go in there,
you're a stranger.
Nothing in there,
except for danger.

Even in the light,
It doesn't add up right,
House Full of Secrets.

Rumours all you ever hear,
Black rain from the skies,
All the versions never clear,
except for all the lies.

JOE WECKERLE

I must admit I've been inside,
but I never stayed the night.
Took all my pride to catch a ride,
from the darkness to the light.

Don't go in there,
you're a stranger.
Nothing in there,
except for danger.

About the Author

Joe Weckerle has a Master's degree in Clinical Psychology from the University of Central Florida and counsels troubled children. He is a screenwriter and producer with a feature film and several TV series and documentaries to his credit. He is also a musician, singer, and songwriter, and his EP *Well-Versed* is available for download on iTunes.

Joe currently lives in Malvern, PA with his wife and children.

Made in the USA
Lexington, KY
10 January 2017